13 Ho

Storyline

Libya, 2012. At an unofficial CIA base in Benghazi a group of ex-military contractors are providing security. In the aftermath of Gaddafi's downfall a power vacuum exists and the climate is volatile. Military weapons are freely available. The US Ambassador to Libya, Chris Stevens, makes a visit to the area, staying in a compound near the CIA base. On the night of 11 September, 2012, the Ambassador's compound is attacked by hordes of heavily armed locals. The only forces willing and able to defend it are six CIA contractors.

BARACK OBAMA: This marks the end of a long
and painful chapter for the people of Libya,

who now have the opportunity
to determine their own destiny

in a new and democratic Libya.

FEMALE REPORTER:
Warring gangs continue to raid

Gaddafi's abandoned armories

as a battle rages in Libya's
two largest cities.

(GUNFIRE)

(INDISTINCT RADIO CHATTER)

(INDISTINCT CHATTER CONTINUES)

(PA BEEPS)

(PILOT SPEAKING ARABIC)

(INDISTINCT CONVERSATIONS)

TYRONE: It's loaded.

- How's the team here?
- Good

Three ex-Marines, one ex-Army Ranger.

It's nice having another team guy around.

Good to see you, brother.

Good to be back.

Oh, man, it's hot!

TYRONE: How are the kids, Jack?

JACK: They're good.

They send their love.

Can you believe Emily's
about to start kindergarten?

She dating yet?

- You better watch your mouth.
- (CHUCKLES)

TYRONE: I thank God I got three boys, man.

You're in for a rough ride, Jack.

Payback's a bitch
and her stripper name is Karma.

JACK: You come up with that on your own?

I saw it on a T-shirt in Mexico.

(LAUGHS)

TYRONE: Hey, check this out.

Remnants of the revolution, man.

Is Becky still mad at me
for dragging you into contracting?

Oh, come on.

She's mad at me, she's not mad at you.

(RONE LAUGHS)

I'm part of the old crowd, the old Jack.

The new Jack
carries a diaper bag instead of an M4.

Is this coming from Tyrone Woods,
dental nurse, who works for his wife?

TYRONE: Guess what? Not out here, brother.

How's the real estate business?

Pretty bad.

How bad is that?

I'm here, aren't I?

TYRONE: Well, this place sucks, Jack.
Not only is it hot as balls,

but you can't tell the
good guys from the bad guys.

(MEN ARGUING)

Shit. No, no, no, this isn't good.

(WOMAN SCREAMING)

Fuck!

Who the fuck are these guys?

What do we got?

The brigade we coordinate with
is the February 17th Martyrs.

This ain't them.

(TIRES SCREECHING)

Shit, we're boxed in.

(PEOPLE CLAMORING)

Are we bailing?

Base, this is Rone.

This is Rone. Come in. Over.

This is base. Go, Rone.

TYRONE: I'm in a jam off Fifth Ring Road.

I'm looking at about eight armed Tangos here.

Copy that. Sit tight.

TYRONE: "Sit tight." That's great advice.

They got a KPV.

Base, we ain't got all day.

KRIS: Hey, Rone. They're trying to get
Feb 17 to back you up, but we're coming.

Hey, Oz, I'm in a jam off Fifth Ring.

Ty.

- (WOMAN CRYING)
- (MEN SHOUTING INDISTINCTLY)

Rone, 17 Feb QRF is being alerted.

Fuck that.

The only Quick Reaction Force
I want is my guys.

No. Contact 17 Feb QRF.

TYRONE: Send them! I want my guys.

Tell them they're not allowed
to leave the base.

Negative, Rone. Just hang in there.

Maybe I'm not making myself clear.

I'm looking at multiple radical insurgents
with AK's and a .50-cal technical

set to blow my Rover
all the way back to Zimbabwe. Over.

It's not my call, brother.

- Here we go.
- (GUN CLATTERS)

(SHOUTS IN ARABIC)

Welcome to Benghazi.

TYRONE: Salaam.

Libyan visa.

Official. Libyan government.

Friendly? Hmm? Friendly?

CLERIC: Pull over for inspection.

No.

Pull over for inspection!

I'm sorry, sir, I can't do that.

(SHOUTS IN ARABIC)

Look up.

Go ahead, look up. You see the drone?

No? That's all right,
because the drone sees you.

Sees your face.

We know who you are.

If anything happens to us, your home,

your family, boom, gone.

Give the order to let us go.

I want the car!

No, I'm not gonna do that.

CLERIC: Look,

I earn right to decide

the future of my country.

You're talking to the wrong guy.

How willing are you to die for your country?

I'm ready to go, right here, right now.

Leave here while you still can.

(SHOUTING IN ARABIC)

(JEEP ENGINE STARTING)

We got air support?

We don't have any fucking support.

Check the new rides. Gaddafi had
a going-out-of-business sale

on armored vehicles.

(WHISTLES) Max-level armored, man.

We got a great deal.

We stole them.

Sat unattended at the airport.

Hey, Chief!

I don't want to hear it, Tyrone.

Oh, no, no, I understand.

I see what you're going for here.

Secret spy base
with fortified walls, gate cameras,

and blue-eyed Westerners walking
in and out of this place all day long.

But if you want to avoid...

That's so rude.

Can't believe he just did that to me.

(BUZZES)

Chief, if you want to avoid
an international incident,

you give me my guys when I ask for them!

Local faces need to resolve
local conflicts, Tyrone.

We're guests in this country.

TYRONE: We're unwanted guests, Bob.

CHIEF: We're spies, you're security guards.

Your job is to keep us out of trouble,
not get into it yourselves.

Well, then help me do my job
and give me my guys.

Here's what you guys are good at.

Working out, eating five hot meals a day.

What you're not so good at

is doing what you're told.

Uh, I need your trace report
on yellowcake in five minutes.

It's coming.

That roadblock was run by Ansar al-Sharia.

It's not just tribal groups
and freedom fighters anymore.

If you have useful intel,
Tyrone, put it in a memo.

You guys bunk here,

but you're not CIA.

You're hired help.

Act the part.

Where are my manners?

Jack Silva, this is our
esteemed Chief of Station.

CHIEF: Hey, Tig. How are the twins?

- Crazy cute.
- CHIEF. Cute.

You have a move tonight.

No recon, Chief?

What makes you Special Operators so special

if you can't do what I need when I need it?

He's fun.

OZ: Well, that was fun.

He gets his jollies
pushing around alphas because he can.

We had this commander back in Ranger school,

he was a real cockbag.

So on our last night, me and a buddy,
we stole his beret.

The whole barracks chubbed it.

- "Chubbed it"?
- Yeah, rubbed our dicks on it.

(MEN LAUGHING)

Leader was a former Gitmo detainee.

Yeah, those guys usually don't hold a grudge.

Jack. Mark Geist.

- Oz.
- Pleasure.

Oh, brother, I'm sorry.
Everybody, this is Jack Silva.

It's our third contract together,
so he knows the drill.

We met training SEALs at Coronado.

How do you get them to balance
that beach ball on their nose?

It's tough.

So we got three ex-Marines here
and one ex-Army retard

who likes to rub his dick on things.

Kris Paronto. Call me Tanto.

Hey, man. I'm Tig.

Tig's been here the longest,
so he'll get you up to speed on the area.

This is Boon. Scout Sniper, Zen Master,

holder of Tanto's leash.

Welcome to Club Med.

So it hasn't rained since June,
it's not gonna rain again until September.

You're double-bunked.
Not me, because I'm in charge.

The gym sucks, food's actually good.

And the Base Chief is kind of a tool.

Well, he's a dick today.

Maybe he just needs a new hat.

TYRONE: Don't encourage him.

Oh, come on. He's a guy with a job to do.

He's playing his string out,
but you talk to him,

Bob did some shit back in the day.

All right, Jack, this is the whiteboard

that's gonna run your life
for the next 60 days.

I want you to check it every hour,

because last-minute moves
pop up every minute, such as

we're shotgunning it in three hours. Mmm-hmm.

(ALL GRUMBLE)

TYRONE: Three hours.
I'll let you know when I'm briefed.

TIG: This was a private family compound

owned by a wealthy Libyan
who got out of town after the revolution

and leased it to the CIA.

He was smart.

(EXHALES)

A little pungent.

TIG: Mmm-hmm.

A little spy tradecraft.

Who'd expect Americans to be hiding out next to a stank-ass slaughterhouse?

We call it Zombieland.

Building A, B, C, D.

- Hesham!
- HESHAM: Yes, sir.

Yes, sir.

Thank you. Thank you, sir.

He's a good man. But there's a few we got our eyes on, so always stay strapped.

(WHISTLING)

(EXPLODES)

Damn kids!

(CHILDREN LAUGHING)

(INDISTINCT CONVERSATIONS)

TIG: This is the bathroom.

This is you.

That's me.

This curtain is meant to discourage you from spooning with me. So...

EMILY: Daddy, what do you do
when you go away for work?

Can't you work here?

- We could have a treehouse business.
- Mmm-hmm.

That sounds amazing.

EMILY: Then we could always be together.

You know, the girls don't need
a treehouse, Jack.

They need you.

I just hope that one day,
you're not gonna wake up and realize

you missed the best part of life.

CHIEF: You contractors
are all married with kids,

yet none of you wear wedding rings.
Why is that?

Our job is reading people.

So, we can't give anyone an edge,
especially bad guys that might use it.

I know you and Tyrone
go way back, so I'll be frank.

The company thinks
you should be here. I don't.

Truth is, there is no real threat here.

We won the revolution for these people.

The more guns there are here,

the more likely there is
to be a misunderstanding.

This is my last station before retiring.

I don't need a misunderstanding.

Is that clear?

Loud and.

These are your credentials,
two weeks per diem.

I'd spend them quick.
Things change fast here in Benghazi.

We have the brightest minds from the Farm,

educated at Harvard and Yale,
doing important work.

Best thing for you to do
is stay out of their way.

TYRONE: Fuck!

Quiet!

You act like animals!

(SPITS)

TYRONE: It's a CPU at Pepe's.

It's all pretty simple stuff, guys.

Public meet.

Libyan oil company exec and his wife.

Case Officers Vayner and Jillani.

Jillani's been developing
this guy for months.

"Developing" is their
new tech word for spy shit.

Jack, since this is your first time with us,
you're gonna be posing as Jillani's husband.

Uh-oh.

I rode bitch last week.

She's a little spicy.

Oz, Tig, limo. Boon, Tanto, follow.

You?

I drive.

TYRONE: Hey, Jack, this is Sona,
she's an American who grew up in France,

which makes her really friendly.

Nice to meet you.

Careful, Jack,

I think she's flirting with you.

(LAUGHS)

BRIT: (SIGHS) Okay.
Let's keep the make-nice to a minimum.

I want to hook this guy tonight.

SONA: He wants to work with us.

Move too fast and you'll frighten him off.

I know how to do this!

He's new.

Not to this.

I don't understand.

Why do they keep
changing security guards on us?

They think we need babysitting.

BRIT: Okay. So just drink your coffee.
Don't try to help.

Don't talk, either.

My name is "Nazia,"
a lobbyist for Exxon Mobil.

Brit is "Peter," my boss.
And you're my husband, "Jack."

Hang on.

Jack's my real name.

It is?

- Fantastic.
- (SONA GROANS)

It's nice to see you again, Fahreed.

Let me introduce you to my boss, Peter.

- Hi.
- Hello.

And this is Jack, my husband.

How are you? Very nice to meet you.

This is my wife.

Nice meeting you.

FAHREED: Oh.
This is the best Italian restaurant. Come.

BRIT: Oh, fantastic.

FAHREED: Please, after you.
SONA: Thank you.

Hey.

What's up?

Hey, Oz. They're in. You got eyes?

Yeah, just enjoying
a little Italian beanery here.

You wouldn't know a good coffee bean
from a lump of squirrel shit, country boy.

Just make sure you pick me up a bag of

that whole bean Arabica Intenso
on the way out.

Fahreed, you can contact us
with this phone in the future.

Good.

BRIT: And if you give me
a call in three days,

I would love to see the manifest,
and we can go over the details.

- Very good.
- Perfect.

(CELL PHONE VIBRATING)

Hey.

What's the Chief's number-one rule?

Don't get out of the car?

No, I'm getting out of the car.

He's on the move.

BRIT: Cairo is great!

Now, that is an underrated city.

What I really love is the Nile Valley.

The Nile Valley is beautiful.

Yes, it's beautiful, but it's too busy.

We had a bit of a fight this morning.

SONA: (CHUCKLES) No, we didn't.

Good price. Two. Two, sir. Good price.

The rocket.

Russian rocket.

Come on, Oz, pick up the phone.

BRIT: We are weighing
a serious move on the Syrian market.

We got to go.

SONA: So, that's why
we really need your shipping support.

Sorry to rush off. Babysitter.

I'm so sorry, but we will be in touch.

Sorry again.

Let's go. Go, go, go.

(BRAKES SCREECHING)

(HONKING)

Go, go, go.

Go, go, go. Get in.

Don't you ever handle me like that again!

Who the fuck do you think you are?

BRIT: You never get out of the car, ever!

You just fucking blew that meet.

Picked up a tail.

See the green van? That's your tail.

Shake and bake!

Green van behind you. We're on it.

Make a left, then another left.

Whoa, whoa, whoa...

This is my second war tour!
I know what I'm fucking doing.

Well, this is my 12th.

If they got pictures of us,
then we need to get them.

I would love to, but that's not our job.

"Protect, not engage." The Chief's orders.

JACK: Got 'em right behind.

Whoa, whoa, whoa...

Get out of the fucking road!

- Oh, careful.
- Rone, coming up on your left!

Excuse me.

Pardon me. Switch sides.

KRIS: He's on you tight, man.
He's getting aggressive.

Yeah. I see him. I see him.

Jack, if he gets too close, drop him.

Watch out!

(TIRES SCREECHING)

I might not have gone to Harvard,
but I'm pretty sure that was a tail.

Hey, guys.

- Hi, Daddy!
- Hi, Daddy!

Hey! Good to see you.

Guys, guys, take a look. Meet my new friend.

- Isn't he cool?
- BEVERLY: Ew It's gross!

He is a grand master at catching flies.

All day, he just sits here
and grabs one at a time.

Are you gonna shave your beard, Daddy?

Well, depends on what Mommy thinks.
Beck, what do you think?

BECKY: Very handsome.

JACK: How's kindergarten, Em?

EMILY: Today is my turn to feed Winston.

Very cool, very cool.

Who is Winston?

- EMILY: He's the class goldfish!
- Oh.

Mommy says I can bring him home one weekend.

Be nice to have a man around the house, huh?

- Okay.
- EMILY: Can we go play now?

RONE ON RADIO: GRS meet in the team room.

BECKY: Is everything okay?

Babe, I think I got to go.

Was that Ty?

It's just a muster call.
It's probably nothing.

- (STAMMERS) Okay
- Sorry.

Just tell the girls I say
I love them, all right?

I'll call you tomorrow.

I love you. Bye.

Silva! You're fucking late! As usual.

Glen Doherty. (CHUCKLES) What's up, brother?

Rone said you were in Tripoli.
What's the occasion?

Ambassador Chris Stevens
is coming in from Tripoli

Monday morning.

JACK: Well, you'll be home.

Not anymore. Three of us extended.

The Ambassador is staying at the Special
Mission Compound at his own insistence.

I know I know it's a problem.

And here's the thing.

The Ambassador isn't
some dilettante political appointee.

He's the real deal.

A true believer.

He's there to win hearts and minds.

Now, he can't very well do that
operating out of a classified facility

that doesn't officially exist.

KRIS: If he's racking
at the consulate with his State detail,

then what fuck does this have to do with us?

He's traveling with no staff,
just a two-man security team.

Now, the State guys
don't know the city like you guys do.

The Ambassador insisted on local drivers,

but we won that argument.

- So we're chauffeurs now.
- Yeah.

Highly trained, highly paid chauffeurs.

Chief won't go for it.
He doesn't want us doing anything.

He didn't go for it. But he got outranked.

Now, the Ambassador deserves the best,

and that's GRS, right?

Hey. Right here. These dudes.

Bad guy house your tail van got towed to.

(CAMERA CLICKS)

Yeah, smile, motherfuckers.

It's just two blocks from the compound.

ALEC: Whoa, whoa, whoa, whoa, whoa.

All right. Hey, what's the problem?

(MEN CLAMORING)

First of all, tell them to calm down.

Everybody, dial it the fuck down!

All right, what is the problem?

17 Feb. These guys look like fun.

There will be no striking. All right?
Get back to work.

How would you feel if you had to
protect Americans at $28 a day

and then bring your own bullets?

Well, why leave security
to the professionals, right?

Gentlemen!

Welcome to the casa.

You guys picked the wrong month
for a bad mustache competition.

Hundred bucks on the line.

Got this one in the bag.

- Scott Wickland.
- Tyrone Woods.

Dave Ubben.

Come on. Let me give you the grand tour.

Huh? (CHUCKLES)

TIG: I can relate.
KRIS: Wow.

OZ: It's like the lobby at Caesars.

- Damn!
- Shit's bangin'.

(SIGHS) Makes you forget you're in Benghazi.

Hey, guys. I'm Agent Alec.

Just dealing with some
Middle Eastern Keystone Cops

out at the gate.

Those guys yell a lot.

What's your setup here?

Our Ambo's residence
in this half of the villa is the safe haven.

Forced-entry, blast-resistant door.

Security bars on the windows.

Inside that is our safe room.

Ambo have any tactical experience?

Nah. He has us.

SCOTT: So, it's a nine-acre
compound, shotgun style

from here,

all the way to the back.

I'll take you there.

His room links to State in D.C. and Tripoli.

JACK: That's the TOC?
SCOTT: Yeah.

Back gate?

DAVE: One way only. Emergency exit.

Got a couple 17 Febs on detail, cameras.

It's locked.

What kind of firepower
you guys carry other than assault rifles?

We've got multiple small arms.

And ammo in the TacOps Center
just beyond the cantina.

That way.

That's it?

I thought every embassy had standard
hard-target security measures.

Car bomb barricades, full-time Marines.

Supposed to.

This isn't an embassy.

We're a temporary diplomatic outpost.

Uncle Sam's on a budget right now,

so I guess normal
security regulations don't apply.

Man, that's some real "dot-gov" shit, huh?

SCOTT: It's like our own little resort.

I hate to piss on your party, ladies,
but five dudes with M4s is not enough.

The locals on your front gate are worthless,

perimeter's soft,

and this whole compound's
a fucking sniper's paradise.

Any big element gets inside here,
you guys are gonna fucking die.

Well, that's heartwarming.

KRIS: What?

No offense.

Guys, we're a mile down the road.

Anything goes down, you call us,
I send Boon, you're good.

JACK: Take care, guys.

What do you think?

A dozen years of military
experience between them, max?

Gonna be a fun week.

Djibouti, request retasking ScanEagle.

DRONE OPERATOR: Copy that.
I have eyes on both.

TYRONE: Oz, sniper over-watch.
Get in position.

Amahl, you lived here all your life, right?

Yes.

Is it true Gaddafi only hired females

for his personal security detail?

Yes. That is accurate.

(LAUGHING)

Gaddafi might've been an evil asshole,
but he wasn't stupid.

(SPEAKING ARABIC)

I hate this part.

Here we go, guys.

Oz, let's rock.

(BOTH SPEAKING ARABIC)

OZ: I got the skinny on the right.

Let me take the whack-out guy.

(BOTH CONTINUE SPEAKING ARABIC)

Amahl, tell this guy to calm down.

Easy, easy.

AMAHL: He's saying bring your weapon down.

He wants his money.

Okay, okay.

This is your money.

TYRONE: Amahl, tell this guy
to calm the fuck down.

That guy's whacked.

Your money.

KRIS: Hey, big man!

(SPEAKING ARABIC)

Whoa, whoa, whoa. Hey, hey! Jambo.

You know the jambo, yeah?

Come on.

AMAHL: Okay, cool down. Okay?

Cool, baby.

Come on.

OZ ON RADIO: That guy almost lost his head.

TYRONE: Base, we are good.

KRIS: Mercenaries all know the jambo, Amahl.

These guys are all right.

TIG: Base, we're looking
at a lot of Russian SA-7s.

Tell him to maintain eyes on the truck
as long as he can.

We're gonna find his stash
and we're gonna level it with a Hellfire.

Hi. Hi, Chris Stevens.

- Sona.
- Sona, nice to meet you. Bob.

- CHIEF: Thank you for doing that.
- It's my pleasure.

- It means a lot.
- So good to be back.

CHIEF: This is our CDOB, Alan. Brit Vayner.

Alan, Chris Stevens. Brit, pleasure.

Gentlemen, greetings. Chris Stevens.

Pleasure to meet you, Mr. Ambassador.

Nice to meet you. Step on in.

AMBASSADOR: So between what
we see happening in Egypt with Morsi

and the current destabilization of Syria,

yes, it's easy to imagine

any number of scenarios playing out here.

However, in my mind,

our biggest mistake would
be to not view this moment

as an opportunity.

Relationships between
governments are important, yes,

but relationships between people

are the real foundation of diplomacy.

And I believe
that it is our mission as Americans

to help Benghazans form a free,

democratic and prosperous Libya.

(SCATTERED CLAPPING)

- (LAUGHING)
- (APPLAUSE)

Okay. Thanks.

In my office, now.

CHIEF: Don't bother apologizing. I'll do it.

Well, I won't.

'Cause I've heard the rah-rah
speech about politics and progress

a hundred goddamn times before.

Well, then I'll write you up.

Sweet.

Chief. Chief,
the guy's going on two hours sleep.

He had a late scout last night
and an early buyback this morning.

Yeah, buying up all of Gaddafi's arms.

Let's count the fucking sand particles
on the beach while we're at it.

Those 30 Grails
that you took off the black market,

that's 30 airplanes that don't go down.

I'm so sick of your shit, Tanto.

If you can't figure out
how to act like a professional,

there are 10 guys waiting to take your spot.

And I'm sure that you'll be happy at home
being an insurance adjuster.

That's the last chance, Tyrone.

TYRONE: All right. GRS,

the Ambassador has
a private meet at the Mayor's office.

So, we're looking at a low-profile event.

We're here to back up State,
so just stay in the background.

SCOTT: Ambo's entering.
Dave, take right side.

TYRONE: Oh. What is this?
You've got to be kidding me.

JACK: So much for a low profile.

SCOTT: Fuck me. Who let them in?

America is here for you.

We are.

This? This is the shit
that pisses my wife off.

Any one of these people
could klack off a vest.

At least it'll be quick, brother.

Don't be an asshole.

AMBASSADOR: A number of countries
have come forth and offered loans,

most recently Turkey.

(INDISTINCT CONVERSATIONS)

AMBASSADOR: Thank you, gentlemen.

Sir. Are we clear on tomorrow?

(EXHALES)

I have been persuaded
in an abundance of caution

to remain inside the compound walls all day,

given the 9/11 anniversary,
so no drivers needed.

Good night.

Hey.

These militias, they have unlimited firepower

and they can coordinate.

You've got to keep his moves low.

Yeah, it was supposed to be closed door.

Someone from the city council
tipped the media.

Sean Smith,

meet Rone, Jack and Tig from the annex.

- Hi.
- How you doing?

Sean was sent here
to install secure comms for the Ambo.

Ended up supercharging our Wi-Fi.

Wish he could do that at our residence.

I got security clearance.

Maybe later this week I'll come by.

SCOTT: Gentlemen, we should be good here.

Call you later to check in.
Have a nice day off.

- How'd it go?
- He's a rock star.

Everybody in Benghazi knew he'd be there.

KRIS: Oh, wait, no, no.
This is it. This is it.

This is Downey's line. Hold on.

Me? I know who I am!

I'm just a dude playing
a dude disguised as another dude.

- Classic.
- (LAUGHING)

(FLY BUZZING)

From the U.S. Department of State.

"Be advised. Reports that a Western facility

"or U.S. installation may be
attacked in the next week."

Read and destroy.

(PRAYERS PLAYING OVER LOUDSPEAKERS)

AMBASSADOR: It is so nice to
be back in Benghazi.

Much stronger emotional connection...

Green, spacious, beautiful compound.

Reconnected with February 17th...

Security is a big concern.

Saw people taking photos
of the compound today,

Feel unsafe here. My guys are concerned.

...guns at arms bazaars...

Voiced it to Tripoli.

It's crazy,

Hey, Nick?

It's the second time I've noticed it.

SCOTT: Hey, Nick, Dave? See if Feb 17 saw anybody at the back gate.

Well, get somebody who speaks Arabic so we can ask them a question.

(INAUDIBLE)

Yeah, come on, put her on the phone.

Oh! Hey, baby.

Kid's discovered she likes Doritos.

(HOWLING)

(LAUGHING) Yeah!

Yeah, that's okay.

You can eat it. You can taste it.

Yeah, buddy, look at your eyes.

Look at that. Who does he look like?

What?

Daughter's drinking.

You drank when you were 15.

Little girls don't drink.

Disneyland? How lucky are you guys?

- What are you guys gonna ride?
- EMILY: Jumbo.

JACK: Dumbo, not Jumbo. Dumbo.

Em, did you thank Mommy? Say thank you?

- Yes, we did.
- Yes.

JACK: I don't think you did.

Huh? Yeah, I'll show them. Hold on.
Baby, that's not me.

That's mean. Look at this.

NARRATOR: ...mate for
1.2 seconds and the act is complete.

(ALL LAUGHING)

KRIS: Why would you send that?

Anyway, if it was, it'd be
the best three seconds of your life.

We miss you. Be safe. We love you.

Yeah, I love you, too.

(LAUGHING) What's he doing?

I want to eat those fleshy arms! Come on!

BECKY: What about the life insurance?

- This is the second notice.
- (SIGHS)

You gotta... You got to pay it.

Okay, okay, I'll figure it out.

JACK: And what are we doing
about the oak tree in the front lawn?

The removal's $700...
No, it's $1,200, not $700.

The guy's trying to rip me off.

Becky, Becky, listen.
I'll be home in two weeks. Okay?

So I'll take it down myself.

Then we're really gonna need life insurance.

(JACK LAUGHS SARCASTICALLY)

(LAUGHING)

I know, I'm...

I'm trying. I'm coming home soon.

MAN: Welcome to McDonald's.
CHILDREN: McDonald's!

- BECKY: Guys, chill out! Turn it down!
- (ALL CHEERING)

Calm down. Mommy's driving. Okay?

We'll take 25 Happy Meals, please!

BECKY: No, we don't want 25 Happy Meals.

Sir, can you just hang on one more second?

We're so hungry!

BECKY: I know you are. Just hold on.

But we want the toys.

Just give me whatever you want.
Six of whatever.

I've got six hungry kids.

- MAN: We don't do that here.
- Throw it all in there.

Daddy, we're having a baby!

- JACK: What?
- Oh, Emily!

Becky, what did she just say?

(CHUCKLES NERVOUSLY)
A baby. We're having a baby.

- Another baby?
- A baby,

MAN: How many Happy Meals did you want?

You can give me
whatever you want! I don't care.

MAN: Chicken McNuggets or cheeseburgers?

44

BEVERLY: We're having a sister!

(CRYING) No, that's it, please.

FEMALE REPORTER: About 1,500 people gathered

outside the American Embassy here in Cairo...

So, anything new back home?

...to voice their discontent and anger

about an American-made amateur film

they say is insulting
to the Prophet Muhammad.

No?

Nothing?

Good talk.

They say that although it's amateur,

it is very much insulting

toward the prophet Muhammad
and that is their red line.

(CAMERA CLICKING)

(DANCE MUSIC PLAYING)

Ooh, ooh!

What up?

- Heard about Cairo?
- Mmm-hmm.

- (LOWERS VOLUME)
- Ah!

Enlighten me, Boon.

"All the gods, all the heavens,

"all the hells are within you."

- TYRONE: Within me?
- Within you.

- I might have to think about that one.
- KRIS: Ooh, ooh!

- Be here all night.
- All right.

Ooh, ooh!

You know, I do have
a gun in my cubby and I will use it.

SOLDIER: Good luck.

She's having dinner with her contact.
We'll be back at 2200.

Yeah.

Well, I'm still waiting to hear back
from State on that.

(FEMALE NEWS ANCHOR SPEAKING ARABIC)

(MAN SPEAKING ARABIC ON LOUDSPEAKER)

(ALL SHOUTING IN ARABIC)

Hey, listen, I just wanted to say
I'm sorry about today.

I don't know what I was thinking.

I guess with what we got going on,

I just wanted everything
to be right, you know. I...

I just wanted to do it right, but

I'm so happy. I...

I can't believe it.

Um...

I miss you guys very much.

I wish I was home.

(STAMMERS) I just wish I was home.

(MEN SHOUTING INDISTINCTLY)

It'll knock your teeth out.

This is some good guava shisha.

Yeah, I got you.

- (ENGINE STARTS)
- (TIRES SCREECH)

(GUNFIRE)

Is that the front gate?

Holy fuck!

Go jock up!

(GUNFIRE CONTINUES)

(MEN YELLING INDISTINCTLY)

SCOTT: I'm getting the Ambo!
ALEC: I'll take the TOC!

Follow me, Vinnie! Watch your six.

What's going on?

(MAN YELLING IN ARABIC)

Chris! Get your body armor on!
Get into the safe haven! Go!

Go!

Hurry!

(PANTING)

Oh, my God. They're everywhere.

What should we do?

SCOTT: Where's the M4?

Sean!

Dave, get your weapon and move fast to villa.

DAVE: How many?

ALEC: All DS be advised, there are thirty...

(BREATHING HEAVILY)

...maybe 40 Tangos coming
through the Charlie-1 gate.

Hello?

Hello?

It doesn't work. Phone! I need a phone!

SCOTT: Alec, call the CIA, call the annex!

RONE ON RADIO: GRS, all GRS,
muster in the CP right now

(SIGHS) I thought it was
gonna be a peaceful night.

(GUNFIRE IN DISTANCE)

TIG: State's under attack!

State's under attack! Let's go, man.

DS Scott, do you have hands on the Ambo yet?

Moving package and guest in the safe haven.

Get down there.

No, I need more information than that.

What do we got, Chief? How many?

Twenty to 40 attackers.

State personnel separated
in several positions.

(DISTANT GUNFIRE)

What's that?

I hear AKs.

RPGs.

That's not good.

- What do I do?
- Get back down!

We're going back.

What's going on out there?

TYRONE: Listen up.

None of you have to go.

But we are the only help they have.

Two vehicles, staged and ready.
Let's go! Move! Move!

Are they coming in?

Jesus! There's nowhere to hide!

Get in the other room! Go!
Get in the other room!

(PANTING)

Tripoli?

Tripoli, Benghazi is under attack.

The Ambo is in the safe haven.

We are overrun.

We need immediate assistance.

We need some fucking help!

HICKS: Magariaf pick up the phone yet?

I got Op Center at State in D.C.

U.S. Military AFRICOM holding.

Yes, AFRICOM.

Firing and chanting.

Front gate. Local guards ran.

Twenty to 40 Tangos,
that's a substantial force.

We got to go right now, Chief.

We have no authority at the consulate.

We have no jurisdiction in this country.

We're not supposed to be here.

But we are here.

We're coordinating with 17 Feb.

They're gonna take the point.

Absolutely not.
You have a U.S. Ambassador at risk.

Send us, Chief. You've got to send us.

The Ambassador is in his safe haven
with his body man.

You're not the first responders.

You're the last resort.

You will wait.

We have no military assets in country.

We have two paramilitary
assets in the country.

One just a mile away from the Ambassador.

And the other?

I need a bag full of money
and a flight to Benghazi.

Scott,

there are Tangos right outside your door.

Do not move. Do not make a sound.

(BREATHING HEAVILY)

(MAN YELLING INDISTINCTLY)

(OBJECT CLATTERING)

(GLASSES CLATTERING)

- KRIS: Amahl!
- Yes?

If we link up with 17 Feb,
none of us knows the language.

We need you, man. Come on.

Hey, hey, what?
Tanto, I'm not a combat interpreter!

- I'm not weapons qualified.
- (COCKS GUN)

- What is this?
- Now you're qualified.

Get your helmet and armor. Let's go.

That dude ain't coming back.

Are you actually trying to fuck me over?

No, that's not what
I'm saying at all. Just hold on!

Now, listen to me.

- Losing the initiative, Chief.
- Will you just hold on?

You're losing it.
You understand how that works?

Stand down. Stand down!

Wait for my word!

At least let us get eyes on.
Then we know if we have to intervene.

And if there's an ambush
and you get entrenched?

Who rescues you?

Me?

Oz, you need to listen to me very carefully,

leave now.

You don't go anywhere near the embassy

Pardon the interruption. We need to go.

- We've just started dinner.
- Now.

Goddamn, you guys! Every time I get close...

OZ: Put your head scarf on!

I need your
eyes and your ears, not your mouth.

ALEC: Annex, we have attackers on compound.

We need immediate help. We are under attack.

COMMANDER: Spool up all available SpecialOps.

I want teams mobilized ASAP.

Stage them in Sigonella, Italy.

Have F1 6s ready on my command,

and I want SITREP on all assets in 5 minutes.

MAN: We'll have
eyes on station in 46 minutes.

After ingress, we'll only have 0:45 overhead.

We need to manage his flight.

Keyhole tactics overhead
for close air support.

I'm just learning
we've got a classified CIA base

a mile away full of Americans.

OFFICIAL: POTUS is about to be briefed.

- (GATE RATTLING)
- (ALL SHOUTING)

(COCKS GUN)

It's bulletproof. It's bulletproof.

What's happening?

They might be going away.

(SIGHS)

ALEC: Scott, can you get
the Ambo to an armored car?

KRIS: Let's go! We got to fucking move!

Could be the start of the Holy War.

BOON: You gonna fight
the Holy War in your shorts?

Strong move.

What the fuck are we waiting for?

We're holding.

He's going with Feb 17 again.

He doesn't want to expose the annex.

Fucking mess.

It's like a damn fireworks show over there.

Seriously, guys, if the consulate ordered

a fucking pizza
it would've been there by now.

(WHISPERING) No. Fuck you.

Scott, they are bringing
diesel cans over to the villa.

Scott, they are coming inside.

They're gonna burn you out.

Okay, okay.

Get in the bathroom, crawl.
Go to the bathroom, go!

They are pouring the diesel
right by the door.

No, don't.

Don't you fucking do it.

Don't do it.

Oh, God.

Shit.

(ALL COUGHING)

SCOTT: Get the towels.

Chris, where are the gas masks?

AMBASSADOR: Oh, God.

SEAN: I can't breathe! I can't breathe!

(COUGHING ON RADIO)

SCOTT: It's too much smoke.

Chris, follow me. Follow me. (COUGHING)

See if you can get hold of any other
quick-reaction forces in the area.

Yes.

Follow me! Follow!

(DISTANT GUNFIRE)

KRIS: Jack, how bad?

(INDISTINCT SHOUTING)

ALEC ON RADIO: GRS, where are you guys?

Please help.

They're digging in now, Rone.

We need some air support.

A Spectre gunship, an ISR drone...
American firepower, man.

I know what we need.

Chief! Chief!

KRIS: Twenty minutes now.

It's going from a rescue mission
to a suicide mission.

Let us loose. Lives are at stake.

You are not direct-action elements.

JACK: Chief, think.

You let them take that consulate,

where do you think
the next target's gonna be?

ALEC ON RADIO: Annex, we need your help.

If you do not get here soon,
we are all gonna fucking die.

Amahl, get in the fucking car now. Let's go!

Now! Let's go!

Amahl, stop!
Do not leave this compound, Amahl.

Get in, Amahl. Let's go!

Amahl! You're not cleared to go!

God damn it! None of you are!

Say goodbye to contract work.

You can't put a price
on being able to live with yourself.

ALEC ON RADIO:
Tripoli, we need immediate assistance.

We need fucking help now!

These assholes have no idea
what's coming for them.

Shit. You got to be fucking kidding me.

I lost my contact.

Shit! I can't go if I can't see.

You got to fix this, man.
You got to fix this right now.

Hey, funny man, shut the fuck up.

TYRONE: You know where you're going.

- This ain't funny.
- JACK: Hold up.

Now 17 Feb knows we're coming, right?

And how do we know that's 17 Feb?

Rone, what are you seeing?

TYRONE: We're 300 yards from the front
gate, Chief, but there's a roadblock.

CHIEF ON RADIO: Are they friendlies? Feb 17?

TYRONE: Chief, trying to assess,
but no one's wearing fucking uniforms here.

Come on. Come on.

Oh...

I didn't get here
late just to die in friendly fire.

Use your gun.

Find out who the commander is
and get this organized quick. Go.

Go.

(SPEAKING ARABIC)

Stop!

(SPEAKING INDISTINCTLY)

(GUNFIRE)

Amahl, get cover!

(SCREAMING ON RADIO)

- Chief!
- ALEC: Please help.

OZ: Get the Chief!

- Are they gone? Yeah?
- CHIEF: Yeah.

I had the rest of the staff
cover in their quarters.

Okay, Bob, Bob, listen to me.

I want 100% accountability. All right?

We're gonna harden our defenses here in C.

This is gonna be our fallback.

Hey, lock this building down!
You, you, let's go. Let's go.

Do it.

How can I help?

(INDISTINCT RADIO CHATTER)

We're pushing forward.

Got to move, got to move.

(DISTANT GUNFIRE)

(WOMAN AND CHILDREN SCREAMING)

(SHOUTING INDISTINCTLY)

Eight to 10 Tangos, front gate.

50/50 these guys turn on us and end this now.

Tanto! Let's get up high.

Rone!

This road's a chokepoint.

We'll get established,
let you know when it's clear to advance.

We're getting our heavy weapons. Be back.

Tig, get Amahl.
Tell 17 Feb to lock down this road.

I don't want anybody
coming over here, all right?

- Let's go! Now!
- Roger that.

TYRONE: Check this dude out.

Lucky we got that guy on our side.

- Hey, check these guys.
- Hi.

Hey.

- You 17 Feb?
- Yeah.

Well, shit, come on, let's go.

Four guys is a fireteam, bro.

Just don't shoot us in the back.

AMBASSADOR: Scott!

Chris! Chris!

- AMBASSADOR: I can't breathe.
- (COUGHING)

Chris!

Chris!

(GUNFIRE CONTINUES)

Tango approaching.

TYRONE: Tanto, get back. We gotta move.

Contact, front!

JACK: RPG.

Incoming!

KRIS: Oh, shit!

- Get cover, get cover!
- Move right, move right!

Left! By the trees!

Ty, to the right!

Move, move, move!

JACK: Tanto, move.
KRIS: Go, go, hustle!

TYRONE: We're pushing
forward to the front gate.

Might want to get inside.

Wonder if they can get the Broncos game?

Get high, get high.

I'm too fucking old to be climbing walls.

(GRUNTS)

Come on.

Jesus Christ, get your
gun out of my face, bro. Fuck!

Fucking amateur hour, man.

DAVE: Is he inside? Is the Ambo inside?

Is Sean inside? Scott, think.
Where did you see him last?

Let's get to the top
of this building. Let's go!

Up here we can cross over
to the bigger building.

RONE ON RADIO: Guys, I need your eyes quick.

Copy that, Rone.
We are coming as fast as we can.

TYRONE: Easy I got four Tangos.

JACK: Who the fuck are these guys?

You are Americans?

Yes.

(CROWD CHEERING ON TV)

These guys are watching a soccer game.

Just another Tuesday night in Benghazi.

TYRONE: We need sniper over-watch
fast. You got to move it!

We're blocked by buildings.
We got no vantage point.

Fuck.

Rone, this roost is a bust.
We're gonna keep moving.

TYRONE: Making our way to the front gate.

Feb 17 is rolling with us.

Check those guys on the left.

TYRONE: Tig, technical!
Knock out that technical!

Tig, you got to knock out
that technical right fucking now, man!

Tig, drop that technical or we're dead!

Move, move, move!

KRIS: Rone, we've been
running about a mile so far.

Making it around
to the back gate of the compound.

CHIEF: On the GPS, where are our teams?

They should be coming back this way.

Look, they're right here.

Tanto and Boon
are on Gunfighter Road at the back.

Rone's team is about to enter the front gate.

Hello, Captain America.
I'm fighting for my country.

(SHUSHES)

You're welcome.

Guess we're going in.

State, we're on property!

State, we're coming in! We're on property!

DRONE OPERATOR:
Delta Pred checking in on station.

We'll have eyes on in two minutes.

TYRONE: Hey, talk to me, guys.

Where are they?

DAVE: I looked everywhere. I can't find them.

I think they're still in there.

You got bad guys inside?

We got separated. I can't find them.

- Our guys? How many?
- Two.

(GROANS) God!

It's too hot! Go around that way. That room.

- Over here?
- There.

Chris! Shit.

Jack, come here!

Let's go in.

Ready? Okay, go in.

(BOTH GROANING)

TYRONE: Chris!
JACK: Let's go, let's go, let's go!

(COUGHING)

No one could survive that.

Let's go.

(BOTH GROANING)

TYRONE: Ambo!
JACK: Chris Stevens!

- Ambo!
- Chris!

- Chris!
- Chris!

KRIS: Shit, I got to do more cardio.

(INDISTINCT CONVERSATION)

(INDISTINCT CONVERSATIONS)

Should be bad guys coming out here.

Maybe they already came through.

DRONE OPERATOR: Phantom Cyclops.

I have two friendlies,
IR strobed, back gate of the compound.

Hey, we are coming
over the back gate. Do not shoot.

Hey, those guys we just
passed at the cafe? Are they with us?

- Friendlies?
- No, mister, no.

We're going over the wall.

Yes, sir.

If they shoot at us...

Yes, sir.

- ...you kill them.
- Okay, mister. Okay.

TYRONE: Chris!

Chris!

Chris!

God!

Chris!

Chris Stevens!

(COUGHING)

Tanto, it's like
a goddamn block party out here.

Get in here, dude.

You 17 Feb?

- I'm a commander.
- Good for you.

Once you get all your guys through here,
you got to close this gate, okay?

- Okay? All right.
- Okay.

(SPEAKING ARABIC)

KRIS: Wait. Who are you talking to?

Who's on the phone?

Okay.

I call attackers.
Maybe I negotiate surrender.

Wait. You called the attackers?
You have their phone...

How the fuck do you have their phone number?

I now a good boy.

But I know bad guys.

- What?
- TIG: Tanto, get in here. We need you.

Yeah, dude, I know, I know, I'm coming.

JACK: Follow my voice!

TYRONE: Jack, keep talking!

Ty, follow my voice!

- TYRONE: Okay. Where are you?
- Follow my voice!

(RONE GROANS)

TYRONE: Jack! Jack, I can't see!

JACK: Ty!

(COUGHING)

Go, go, go.

Amahl!

Hey, I brought these 17 guys, okay?

But I do think these

assholes, they were trying to steal our cars.

They were the dudes
who were supposed to take point.

Yeah.

Now, this is fucking bad.

(COUGHING)

KRIS: Rone, we're in the back of
the compound, we're going to the TOC.

Oh, shit.

Jesus Christ, that shit is torched.

Who are these guys?

Whoa.

Soldiers! Americans are in trouble!

Huh?

Your Americans are in trouble!

Go, go, go. Go!

DAVE: Go, go, go.

JACK: Who is it?

DAVE: It's Sean Smith, our IT guy.

Let's go. Hold him up.

(GROANS)

JACK: Tig, med bag!

SCOTT: I was just with him.

I was just with him.

KRIS: GRS moving in on the TOC.

Hey, we're outside the TOC.
Door's locked. Anybody in there? Over.

TYRONE: That's it. He's gone.

- He's gone.
- No!

He's gone. Now is not the time.

- Get yourself together, Tig.
- No.

Don't waste your energy, man. He's gone.

Jack, let's get his body in the vehicle.

Pick him up.

All right, move. (GRUNTS)

Explain to me
how all these guys are friendlies.

Funny, I don't know.

Funny? It's not that funny.

Who are you?

What are you doing,
coming out of the bushes like that?

BOON: Hey, inside the TOC,
do you see us? We need to come in.

You know that thing where the initial assault

is just a ploy to draw people
in for the real attack?

Jesus Christ.

Open your door
or I'm gonna fucking blow it open!

- (SHOUTS IN ARABIC)
- Blue.

BOON: CIA!

Whoa! Hey!

Easy, Forrest Gump! We need you.

Is there anybody else inside?

No, no.

- Glad you're here, brother.

- Yeah, buddy.

Hey. Hey. They're coming back!

They said the attackers are regrouping,
adding reinforcements.

Coming back to finish the job?

Jack, help get State's classifieds
out of the TOC.

I'm gonna get DS out of here.

AMAHL: You better hurry up.

Amahl, follow me. Let's go.

Tanto, we got a situation coming our way.

DS! Get in your car.

JACK: Tanto, blue, blue!

Boon's inside. Go.

(COUGHING)

Jack, what's going on over there?

It's not good. (COUGHING)

We got one KIA.
We got guys still in the bushes.

No Ambo.

They're still here.

I think we got hostiles everywhere.

The fire has just got to be cover.

They have control of the compound.
Why else leave so fast?

Black Hawk Down, man.

They're gonna drag
his body through the streets.

- Amahl. Hey.
- (CRYING)

Amahl, pull it together, man. Come on.

Come here. Stop pointing your gun!

We ready?

On me. Here we go.

Let's go. Amahl, out.

Oh! Goddamn it! This cockbag motherfucker!

Be advised the 17 Feb
tactical genius commander

left the back gate wide fucking open.

All right, Boon,
this wall set as new perimeter.

Take cover, hold it.
We're getting DS out of here.

Let's go! Move!

Go inside, please. Go back inside.

Get in the house right now! In the house!

Fire sale! Everything must go.

We got a large group
of bad guys headed our way.

We're gonna stay and look for the Ambo.
You guys need to exfil.

We're short two guys.

I got two more agents,
and I'm not leaving them.

Hey, Tanto, what's going on, man?
We got to move.

(MEN SCREAMING)

You dumb piece of shit!

You blew yourself up trying to frag us, huh?

17 Feb?

Yes!

Fuck.

Oh, shit!

Boon! Let's go back!

Jack, watch our six!

All right. Listen to me.
Listen, hey. Listen up!

When you go outside that gate,
you go left, you understand?

- Yes.
- You understand?

Haul ass!

Hey! Hey! Hurry up!

Let's go! Let's go! Move, move, move!

Let's move!

To the right is bad guys. You are going left.

You're taking the back way to the annex.

- You got it?
- I got it.

Listen, I think somebody else should drive.

No, I'm driving!

Blue! Blue!

No, don't shoot!

- Move, move, move, move.
- (TIRES SCREECHING)

Second wave is coming!

They're flooding in through the back gate!

Peel it! Peel it! Peel it!

Someone cover us on the roof!

Amahl, on Tig! Let's get these guys out.

I'm on the roof. Don't leave me.

State. We are exfilling
the compound, minus the Ambo.

DAVE: No, no, no, he said go left.

Left!

- Scott, left.
- No, he said right.

Go back the other way.

- Hey, get out of the way!
- Back right.

Left! Go left!

SCOTT: Go! Go!

DAVE: Move, move, move.

SCOTT: Who's this fucking guy?

DAVE: I don't know. Maybe he's 17 Feb.

Maybe he's friendly. Maybe he's saying
go the other way. Go the other way.

JACK: No! Left!

Go left! Go left! Left!

I can't believe we left without him.

JACK ON RADIO: You're going the wrong way.

RONE ON RADIO: Jack, get up here on roof.

JACK: Tig, on your right.

TYRONE: Down road, back gate.

Tangos left.

Hey. No way these guys are in for the night.

They got a little taste of victory.
The annex is next.

Tanto, Boon, consolidate.
Let's get the fuck out of here.

Let's go!

Exfil!

Get that door open!

That was intense.

TIG: I forgot the grenade launcher.

DRONE OPERATOR: We got a mover.
State armored car leaving compound.

AFRICOM OFFICER: Target vehicle
intercept. Downrange 22 degrees.

Stand by for words.

DAVE: We just went in a circle, Scott.

What is this shit?

SCOTT: Who is this?

What is he saying?

This is a bad idea. Just go.

(SPEAKING ARABIC)

DRONE OPERATOR: Target vehicle has stopped.

Tangos converging from all sides.

ALEC: Who the fuck is this guy?
Who is this guy?

Who are you?

He's doing this.
I think he's trying to say he's friendly.

No, we don't know these guys.
This is not safe.

(SPEAKING ARABIC)

ALEC: We don't know them.
We're not safe here.

VINCENT: Two guys on the balcony.
Two guys on the balcony.

We need to get out of here.

DAVE: Who is that?

It's a trap, Dave,
it's an ambush! We've got to move!

(MEN SHOUTING IN ARABIC)

ALEC: He might be trying
to keep us from an ambush.

Who are you?

Back up while we can. Back up while we can.

SCOTT: Who are you?

- (CAR ENGINE REVVING)
- (SHOUTING CONTINUES)

Get out of the way! Get out of the way!

(DAVE SCREAMING)

Go, go, go! Push through!

(TIRES SCREECHING)

DAVE: Keep going! Keep going! Keep going!

Go to the right!
Go to the right! Go right! Go right!

VINCENT: Damn it.

(ALL SHOUTING IN ARABIC)

Run them the fuck over!

(GROANS)

(TIRES SCREECHING)

We've got three cars
coming up on our ass fast!

VINCENT: Punch it, punch it!

DRONE OPERATOR:
Light fire pursuit of target vehicle

half-click south of annex.

State. We're under heavy fire!
We're on run-flats!

AK coming up eight o'clock!
This window's not gonna hold!

Shoot that son of a bitch!

DAVE: Shoot him!

(HORN HONKING)

RPG!

Coming in!

(TIRES SCREECHING)

(SCREAMING)

Hey, easy, Rone. Try to blend.

JACK: We are.

With a dead body in the back,
bunch of heavily armed operators

just going back to hide

in our covert CIA base.

Hey, we got a tail.

Two of them.

TIG: Annex, we got a tail.
Two or three vehicles in pursuit.

Start the destruction phase.
Plan to evacuate.

KRIS: Hit it, Rone.

How we looking?

- You lost them, Rone.
- You lost them. You're good.

- You sure?
- Yep. Yep.

That's because he knows where we live.

Guard, get in the tower!

Chef, you ready to get in the fight?

Anyone comes over these walls tonight,
we're kicking some ass.

ALEC: Keep moving. Keep moving.

VINCENT: Contact rear! Go, go, go, go!

DAVE: We're coming in hot.

We're closing in at about 100 meters.

OZ: Let's go! Shut the gate!

(COUGHING)

Hey! Hey, get back inside! Get back! Now!

Go back inside.

Vinnie, give me a hand.
Let's get him to medical.

- Go. Take him.
- (COUGHING)

Does that need attention?

No, no. I'm good. It's a flesh wound.

Let me do something to help.

I need men east side. Take Building D.

We need all the help we can get. Let's go.

You guys got the gate? Gate!

(TIRES SCREECHING)

Hey. I had extra ammo
brought up to the rooftops.

Libyan guards are positioned in the towers.

Should've turned left.

Get some water and reload!

Who's gonna bring him inside?

TYRONE: He stays right here, Chief.

When we exfil out, it's gonna be quick.

What about the Ambassador?

No one could survive that.

Right now, we need men on the roof.

I want to make a run for the airport.

Maybe you haven't noticed

it's open season on Americans
in Benghazi right now.

Rone.

Every extra mag loaded now.

Don't take your eyes off
the exterior cameras.

Rone, you realize if we stay here
that we are screwed.

Then why don't you get us
some fucking help, Bob?

Tell AFRICOM you're calling
from that classified base

they didn't know existed until an hour ago.

You be very specific. You get
a Spectre gunship and an ISR Pred.

There is a drone from Derna

85

overhead right now.

The gunship is out of fueling range.

That's what they're telling me.

I'm ordering the evacuation.

You're not giving orders anymore,
you're taking them.

You're in my world now.

I... I tried to find him.

No gunship?

(EXHALES)

Six hours till dawn.
Entire city knows where we're holed up.

When they come,
we're gonna unleash hate on these guys.

Let's set our priorities.

We're gonna continue our base
destruction protocol until it is finished.

We're gonna exfil from here
in 30 to 40 minutes.

We're gonna go directly
to the airport and get a plane.

If that doesn't work, we're gonna go to the
port and we're gonna steal a fucking boat.

If any one of you gets separated
from the group at any time,

memorize this number.

The CIA satellites
will pick you up where you are located.

If there's anyone who has local assets
with friendly militias, raise your hands.

You need to assure me
that those people are safe.

They're gonna secure our exit
and escort us out of here.

Call them right now, immediately.

I want all heads of department over here.

And I want a fucking war room.
We're gonna make our finalized plans.

Now, listen, listen.
You're trained to do this.

It's your job. You can do it.

We're all responsible for our lives,

and what you do right now in this room

will determine whether we live or die.

GLEN: Tripoli, we're here,
getting on the oil executive's jet.

(DOOR CLOSES)

GRS is back safe. Compound's lost.
Still no sign of the Ambo.

State's already blaming Al-Sharia.

You're with Delta? What, just two of you?

We're it, brother.

Okay.

That sucks.

There's our bird! Let's move.

CHIEF: That's supposed
to be a phone number, and it's not.

You need to translate this right now.

Did you get these?

Destroy those.

Listen, listen!
I'm having trouble hearing you,

but our sources are checking every hospital.

CHIEF: Have you alerted the Pentagon
and CIA? Are they talking?

SONA: Amahl!

Amahl, what did you see? Are you hurt?

Amahl, what's happening out there?

- It's so bad. It's not good.
- KRIS: Amahl!

Amahl, can I get my gun?

Sorry, buddy, I think I'm gonna need it.

Shit.

What's the situation out there?

Grab a gun, meet me on the roof.
I'll tell you all about it.

He isn't serious, is he?

'Cause that's his job, that's not my job.

He is serious.

- (BANGING)
- Come on up! Check it out!

Listen up, guys!

I'm gonna take Building C.
Jack, Tig, I want you on Building D.

Building A, Tanto, Boon.
Building B, DS guys, that's your territory.

Oz, Tower 1 . Zombieland.

Let's go. Hit it.

Move!

KRIS: Let's go! Let's go! Let's hustle up!

OZ: Rone, I got the tower! Getting up on C!

They're just the local shepherds.

(SPEAKING ARABIC)

Hey, what's going on?

We got a neighbor at the gate
complaining about our lights.

What, does he think
we're having a pool party?

He says the lights are bad.
They're going to find you.

"They"?

How the fuck does he know
who "they" are? Ask him.

He's already gone.

KRIS: Guys, we really
need to do something about these lights.

We've got to shut all these lights down.

TYRONE: Hey, guys,
keep your IRs pointed up for the gunship

that's hopefully fucking coming.

Time for stealth has passed.

Viper, keep the perimeter floodlights on.

Shut off the interiors.

90

Roger that. Roger that. Come on, come on.

In Iraq, we had Black Hawks
to get us out of shit like this.

Yeah. Well, here we got nothing and no one.

Kill the interior lights!

- We're lit fucking targets up here.
- I'm trying, man.

Hello.

Surreal.

Different world.

Who's this?

Amahl, are those cars coming
from the neighbor's house?

Hey! Where the fuck are they going?

Guys, we just lost all our Libyan security.

Does it seem like everybody knows
what's going on around here but us?

That's for sure.

Strobe's on, marking our position
for the Predator.

I hate to break it to you,

but I don't think we're getting any gunships.

Oh. Hell no. Air support? That'd be too easy.

TIG: Viper, turn off these goddamn interiors
or I'm gonna shoot them out myself!

I'm working on it.

- He's having a bad night.
- Work with me.

- Fuck.
- Come on.

- Oh!
- (CHUCKLES)

Sorry, guys. I'm just a bit nervous.

Wow. Thank you.

BOON: Rone, which way
you think they're coming?

When they come,
they're coming through Zombieland.

That's strange. That cop slowed down,
then sped back up.

KRIS: I feel like I'm in
a fucking horror movie.

- Chef?
- Yeah?

Put that down right there.

You go downstairs, make sure

everybody in this building's safe.

CHEF: Got it.

TYRONE: Oz? This is where we make our stand!

- It's dark out there.
- BOON: Hey, Rone,

we're going to Building B.
It's better vantage.

Get those DS guys off of there.

State!

I want you to go down
and protect Building C from the ground.

OZ: Guys, let's set sectors of fire
with overlapping coverage.

Tig, I can use you over here on Tower 3.

Oz, what do you got?

OZ: I got a couple
of local shepherds walking.

KRIS: Hey, State, we got this.
Lot of acreage out there.

- Get on your NODs.
- Copy that.

Hey, Chief. Are we expecting any
friendlies to set up a perimeter?

CHEF: Uh... Not that I know of. Why?

KRIS: 'Cause we got cars amassing, east side.

In the parking lot out by that house

where the teenagers
are that throw the M-80s over the yard.

Then I guess it could be poker night.

Just hold on.

Hey. I got two cop cars pulling in.

KRIS: Chief, are we expecting
any of Benghazi's finest anytime soon?

CHIEF: Let me check on it. Hold on.

Yeah. Take your time.

Alan, check the perimeter.

Call Benghazi police and see if that's them.

KRIS: Chief, these cops?
I bet you they work for the bad guys.

Does this look like 17 Feb to you?

Dude, how can you fucking tell?

They're all bad guys until they're not.

(SPEAKING ARABIC)

BOON: And there go the cop cars.

I got movement. You see this, guys?

Yeah, I see it.

TYRONE: Boon, how many you see?

I got unknowns moving to the parking lot.

Fifteen Tangos.

I gotta call you back.

OZ: Good vantage point from here.

TYRONE: Oz?

OZ: All right. I got five more guys
right behind them little shepherds.

One of them's got something slung.
I can't see what it is.

TYRONE: Everyone's got weapons in Benghazi.

Until you see a weapon
in someone's hands, you do not fire.

I don't want anybody going to prison.

Roger that.

Okay, they're breaking off. It's game time.

BOON: Guys, they are coming in.

Oh, yeah, they're coming in now. Come on.

Chief, if we're expecting any friendlies,

I need to know that information now.

I am not aware of any friendlies.
I have no confirmation.

DRONE OPERATOR: AFRICOM,
ISR is approaching target coordinates

from deployed strobe tracker.

Await further instruction.

AFRICOM OFFICIAL: ISR, eyes-on report.

DRONE OPERATOR: AFRICOM, unknowns
are advancing toward subject compound

moving from south/southeast over open ground.

No tags or colors. Asymmetrical movements.

No weapons observed.

ISR TECH: Cyclops pushing in at 140.

State, we're being surrounded
by Tangos right now.

Chief, this shit's starting to get real.

Oz, we got seven Tangos by the pillars.

OZ: Got 'em.

Let 'em come.

Let 'em come.

Let 'em come.

KRIS: Chief, are we cleared hot to shoot?

Chief, I repeat, are we cleared hot to shoot?

See a weapon, shooter's discretion.

Everybody hold. You do not
fucking fire till I give the word.

I ain't shooting no kids, Boon.

All right, guys, eyes open.

I'm gonna paint these guys with the
infrared so we're all on the same page.

Everybody got this guy?

BOON: Roger. OZ: Yeah. I got him.

KRIS: This guy?

- BOON: Got him.
- Got him.

KRIS: This guy?

- OZ: Got him.
- BOON: Got him.

- How about that guy?
- Three.

OZ: I see him.

KRIS: Look at these guys.
It's like kids playing hide and seek.

I got AKs.

TYRONE: You guys got to draw them in.

Draw them in. They cannot see you.

We have night vision, they don't.

Turn the lights off now.

KRIS: How much closer do we let them get?

OZ: They got weapons.

Come on, Rone, they're right here.

OZ: We got about 25-30 Tangos.

(ALL SCREAM)

(GROANS)

I'm taking the right side.

OZ: Tig, you hit?

- You all right?
- (GRUNTS)

Armor caught it.

That's a mistake.

Dude, we kicked their asses!

I don't know if I'm feeling lucky or unlucky.

They thought they were walking
into another temporary embassy.

Not here, brother.

KRIS: Chief, get us some air support,
huh? Get us fucking something!

(SNIFFS) GRS, check in.

BOON: All good, Boon, Tanto, Building B.

D was out of the fight.

(PANTING) Tower 3, Tig and Oz, never better.

Let's get you up. Stay down.

BOON: Bad guy's house is still active, Ty.

We got eyes on.

Roger that.

They shot out all the lights.

First wave got the job done.

You want a coffee? I sure as hell do.

OZ: I guess the drone saw
30 guys shooting at us.

(WHISPERS) Come on.

DRONE OPERATOR: Secure
with tech two encryption.

Why is this shepherd walking
around after a gunfight?

So bizarre.

OZ: These sheep freak me out.

Somebody could take a potshot from in there.

I don't think it's safe.

Let's get out of here.

Dave, you got to slow it down, buddy.
You're working too hard.

(PANTING)

Look, this isn't a choice for me.

We lost the Ambassador.

That's on our heads, not yours.

And, look, I get it.
I know what you're thinking.

But if Scott had fired
on that mob from the safe haven,

it would've given away his position.

And we wouldn't have had a fighting
chance in hell to get him out.

So, I'm in this fight. All night.

I know you are.

I get it, man.

(ALL ARGUING IN ARABIC)

Hey! Hey, what's going on?
Where are our rides?

Look, this is all
screwed-up Libyan bureaucracy. Okay.

Who drives, who goes first,
and of course who gets paid the most.

We don't have time for this!
You tell them to figure it out.

Keep a close watch on them.

We don't know who's good and who's bad.

Copy that.

(ARGUING CONTINUES)

We're wheels down, but we got a problem.

What do you got? Coffee.

(DOOR CLOSES)

- Amahl.
- Yes.

Tell him he should assemble his men
as quickly as possible

and that we will pay him.

(SPEAKING ARABIC)

- Cash.
- Cash? Fine.

When? When can they be here?

Where's the Chief?

Just bring... That he brings his fucking men as soon as possible

and get us the hell out of here.

Looting the compound.

Blood in the water. Sharks are circling.

The Tripoli team is stuck at the airport.

They need an escort.
They don't know the city.

(LAUGHS)

(LAUGHS)

No love from the Libyan government?

(LAUGHS) They've gone home for the night.

Or just not answering.

What about ours?

They picking up the phone?

I'm working on it.

That drone feed's up.

They're seeing everything we see and more.

PILOT: We've identified

the forces that can move to Benghazi.

They're spinning up as we speak.

MAN: State has been asked to secure
the approval from the host nation.

General, this could be a hostile airport,
so we are considering every option.

Understood. It's a fluid situation.

But there are a lot of Americans stuck there.

I say we get them airborne,
then we can make our decision.

Hey, Glen, we've been
waiting for three hours.

Can we just commandeer these vehicles and go?

Getting in isn't the problem.
Getting out again is.

Hey!

Can you explain to them

that if this bullshit
ends up costing American lives,

I'm gonna come back here and cut all
their throats myself, starting with him.

You tell him that.

(SIGHS) What a shitshow.

State got a report
from the Benghazi Medical Center

that said a crowd
of Libyans brought in an American male

alive.

They used Scott Wickland's phone,
said it came from Chris' pocket.

Could try and draw us in.

Watch out for an ambush.

What do you see?

(SIGHS)

I'm not sure what it is.

Either the bad guys
are crawling under the sheep

or the sheep are humping.

2:30 at night?

I don't know anything about sheep.

(GROANS)

OZ: Watch your step.

Oz.

OZ: Stay low. Stay low.

I brought you candy bars and some drinks.

Your head.

It's nothing.

You need anything else?

Well,

a lawn chair wouldn't be bad.

Right. No problem.

And a gunship.

I don't think we're gonna
be able to get you that.

I'd settle for a few F1 6s.

Low fly-by over the city would

put the fear of God
and the United States in them.

Buy us a few more hours.

How long can you hold them off?

Any large force with any real ordnance,
I don't know.

You got contacts here and at home?

Start making some calls.

- Hey, the stripper's here!
- (CLEARS THROAT)

- Here are your clothes.
- About time.

How are the Jason Bournes doing downstairs?

Everyone's scared.

I just got a text from my cousin,
you know, a warning,

saying to leave before it's too late.

More good news.

Anything more specific than that?

I don't think we need
an interpreter anymore, Amahl.

You did good. You should go.

No. I'm staying here with you guys.

I'll be downstairs.

(SIGHS)

I'm gonna have to break up
with him before we leave Libya.

(BOON LAUGHING)

JACK: How do you leave me
on D when the party's right here?

Hey, about this whole Ambo story,

I don't buy it.

And if he is still alive,
Glen's team's gonna get him out first.

If they do, they're not gonna get to us.

So we've got to be prepared
to be here for a while.

Chief said it was on the news back home.

Something about street protests.
Anti-Islamic films.

We didn't hear any protests.

It was reported in the news, buddy.

- JACK: Hey.
- (VEHICLES APPROACHING)

You see that?

At the end of Smuggler's Alley. Take a look.

Could be a second front forming.

Or an audience gathering to watch the show.

KRIS: Hey, Chief.

I know you've had some
pearls of wisdom tonight,

but are we expecting any friendlies?

I got a lot of movement out here.

Looks like we're gonna get hit again.

Dave, take Zombieland. Oz, with me.

Grab a shield. Grab a shield.

(BOTH GRUNTING)

KRIS: Chief, tell them
to get the Hellfire on that Pred ready,

Be advised,

ISR saying that cars and bodies are massing

in the parking lot to our west.

KRIS: Yeah, Chief, I just put that out
over the radio about two minutes ago.

Tell the ISR guys
they're pretty much worthless.

Fucking smartass.

(ALL SPEAKING ARABIC)

Come on, come on, come on!

Send.

OZ: Chief, we got 30 guys approaching.

(CLICKING)

Hey. Is that thing loud?

Oh, yeah.

I forgot my earplugs.

TYRONE: Keep your eyes
on your assigned quadrants.

We don't want to get flanked.

You ready, Tig?

- Here we go.
- Watch for different tactics.

Oz?

You lose your tampon?

JACK: Tig, watch the pine trees.

KRIS: What is this?

What is this yo-yo doing?

KRIS: You think they don't know
we have night vision?

TYRONE: GRS, I want everybody to hold.

Thirty yards.

BOON: No, no, no, no. What are you doing?

No, don't do that. Fuck!

Get down!

What? Louder!

CHIEF: Stop! Stop shooting!

17 Feb says you're firing at them!

Somebody started shooting at us first!

And they're still fucking shooting at us!

Tell them to stop shooting at us

and we'll stop shooting at them.

If they're shooting at you,
just fucking shoot back!

That's what I'm telling you!
We got 30 guys firing at us!

17 Feb, my ass.

JACK: Tig, tree line.

OZ: They're flanking us from Zombieland!

- Move!
- Moving!

Upstairs window.

Bus.

We got big ordnance coming out of there.

Hit the bus!

That one's for us.

KRIS: You're not getting away this time!

You think they're losing heart?

SONA: Everyone, over here.

Find me every airbase
in the area that can reach us.

BRIT: Find me any quick response teams,

any Navy carrier battle groups
in the vicinity, now.

(PANTING)

CHIEF: I hear they have
a US CIF team in Croatia.

MAN: That's a two-hour flight.

SONA: Sigonella, Aviano, Benghazi.

- How far is Aviano?
- 700 miles.

There's an F1 6, 365 days 24/7.
It's a quick response base.

Well, bring it in from Sigonella.

It's a fucking puddle jump
from Italy to here.

It's 20 minutes.

SONA: I'm not requesting firepower.

All I want is that you
give these assholes outside our gate

a low, loud "fuck you" flyover.

My authority?

My authority

is that if you don't send,
Americans are going to die.

Including the one talking to you right now.

You see that, dude?
There's guys on those rocks over there.

There's nothing there.

Your eyes are playing tricks, man.
Why don't you go take a break?

(SIGHS) No. I'm okay.

Tig, take a break.

(TIG SIGHS)

TYRONE: Hey, Tig.
Go on down, man. I'll spell you.

Oh, those State guys. (EXHALES)

Dave up on C,
you should see the look in his eyes.

(RONE EXHALES)

These guys are gonna relive this night
for the rest of their lives.

My whole mindset? Never feel that.

You go down shooting, balls out, every time.

How you doing, brother?

Down time's the worst, isn't it?

Adrenaline leaves
and your mind just starts to wander.

Oh, yeah.

I haven't thought
about my family once tonight.

Thinking about them now.

Up here in the middle of all this,

I'm thinking about my girls, man.

Thinking

what would they say about me?

"He died in a place he didn't need to be,

"in a battle over something
he doesn't understand,

"in a country that meant nothing to him."

Every time I go home to Becky
and those girls, I think this is it.

I'm gonna stay.

And then something happens
and I end up back here.

Why is that? Why can't I go home?

Why can't I go home and just stay there?

Warriors aren't trained to retire, Jack.

Becky's pregnant.

You kidding me?

She told me today.

And that can't be the last call.

That can't be the last call,
'cause I'm sitting up here

and I'm thinking about some
other guy raising these girls.

Man, I'm sorry.

- No, no, hey...
- I shouldn't have...

Mmm-mmm. No, man, no... It's all right.

I get it. Okay?

You go to them.

I know what it's like to be
in a place like this,

let another man raise your children.

When I was young,
I was giving myself to something bigger.

Jack, that something bigger's gone now.

(SIGHS HEAVILY)

114

(CHUCKLES)

But your new son?

Kai is your second chance.

I might actually not be a half-bad father.

(BOTH LAUGH)

"All the gods, all the heavens,
all the hells are within you."

What is that?

Something Boon dropped on me earlier.

And it's just been going around
in my head all night.

CHIEF: We have some clarity
on a couple of issues.

The Tripoli team has cleared the airport,
and they are on their way,

You've got to be kidding me. It's about time.

CHIEF: We also have confirmation.

It is Ambassador Stevens.

But the earlier report
that he was admitted alive

was inaccurate.

He was apparently found

in the back of the villa

and brought to the hospital
by a crowd of Libyans.

Cause of death is smoke inhalation.

Shit.

(SIGHS)

You know, we could've saved him

if we'd gone when we got the call.

We could've saved them both.

Yep.

(SNIFFS)

You know, they're gonna get this figured out.

Come at us with technicals next.

We'll have to get down off this roof
and engage them direct.

- Yeah, I know.
- (SIGHS)

I never really get scared.

Is that weird?

Whenever bullets start to fly,
I always feel protected.

You know, like it's...

As long as I'm doing the right thing,
God'll take care of me.

But that's crazy, right?

Not any more than everything else you say.

Hope God has a sense of humor.

Yeah.

I guess we'll find out soon enough.

I had a good call home today.

Yeah?

Talked to my kids.

Me, too.

OZ: Hey, we need somebody on
Building A eyeballing our visitors.

Yep. (GRUNTS) That's me.

You good, brother?

Yep.

Hey, man.

It's been fun, right?

Yeah.

It's been fun.

What, do you mean
they don't know where it is?

Our Libyan friends here aren't much help.

Okay, annex, we're officially lost.

Neither Google or Siri know
where the fuck you are.

Let Tripoli ops know
I'm lassoing our location.

There should be an IR lasso
visible right now.

There. There it is up ahead. I see it.

Man, I could crush some pancakes.

Smothered with butter.
Some of that whipped cream.

Chocolate chips. I'd do any of it right now

KRIS: Hey, guys.

I don't know if this is
an awkward time to tell you,

but I've had to take a crap
ever since we left the consulate.

Way too much information, brother.

KRIS: Hey, Chief.

We're expecting more than one car, correct?

CHIEF: I am not aware
of any friendlies. No word.

I got three Tangos in a car coming up
to the front gate, right now.

Coming in hot.

They stopped.

Come on.

TYRONE: He better have a weapon.

Show me a gun.

JACK: Could be a carbomb.

KRIS: Nope. No gun, just a phone.

I want to shoot this guy, Rone.

Rone, I'm gonna shoot him in the face.

What's he doing? He's turning around.

He's pulling out.

He's taking off.

Could be someone using their cell phone
to get target coordinates.

(SIGHING)

(PRAYING IN ARABIC ON LOUDSPEAKERS)

All right. Weird shit's
starting to happen now.

I've had just about enough of this
2012 Alamo bullshit.

Can we get the fuck out of here now?

(ALL PRAYING IN ARABIC)

(PRAYING STOPS)

I know I blew an eardrum earlier, but

did all the chanting just stop?

That can't be good.

Guys, this sucks. Every Ranger knows

dawn is when the French and Indians attack.

I'm feeling lucky tonight, Tanto.

KRIS: Chief.

Are we expecting some trucks,
or big mounted technicals?

Blue, blue! Cavalry's here!

KRIS: Yeah. You're looking a little light,
but welcome to the party!

Middle East never lets you down.

Personable, organized, easy to navigate.

Makes me need a fucking drink!

Where's my frogman?

KRIS: Building C, up top!

We gonna exfil now?

KRIS: Get us to Tripoli,
brother, I'll get you wasted.

I'm the Commander of the Libyan Shield.

Thank you for coming.

Sir, we're tasked
with sensitive document destruction.

OZ: Not a moment too soon.
TYRONE: Hey, Glen!

GLEN: Anyone call an airport limo?

What's up, brother Bub?

- Good to see you, brother.
- (CHUCKLES)

Sorry I'm late.
I got hung up in the gift shop.

Oh. You guys made a mess up here.

Would've waited for you,

but people crying and dying
over the radio, man.

We didn't have the heart for it.

Hey, Rone, I'd like to tell you
it's over, but it isn't.

The 24 CIA staffers here,

plus five State guys, plus six GRS, plus us.

I get it. Too many.

There's no room in the jet.

You think you can hold things down
here for a few more hours?

I'll tell you what.

These are some hellish warriors.

I'd be lucky to have their back any day.

- Hey, Dave!
- DAVE: Yo.

Lucky day. Head on down.

- Safe travels, buddy.
- Thanks.

I'll grab my gear.

Hey, where's Silva at?

- Over on D.
- Yeah?

JACK: I didn't think you were coming.

Figured you had something better to do.

Dude, I was.

Then there's all that "never leave
a brother SEAL behind" bullshit,

so here I am.

Long ride to the airport ahead of us.
I'll see what the hold-up is.

(MAN SPEAKING ARABIC)

Hey, hey, hey!
Where the hell are you guys going?

Chickenshit!

Guys.

(DISTANT EXPLOSION)

Did anyone else hear that?

Guys, is that a mortar?

TYRONE: Mortars incoming. Get cover!

(DAVE SCREAMING)

I'm hit! I'm hit!

Oz, I'm coming!

(GROANING)

(INAUDIBLE)

(DISTANT GUNFIRE)

(OZ GROANING)

(GRUNTING)

Rone! Rone!

(OZ YELLING IN PAIN)

MAN: This is Langley, Give us your stat.

You okay? Looks bad.

Bob, answer.

Building A, what's going on? Check in.

KRIS: Get Deltas up on the roof now!

DELTA: Blue, blue. Going external.

Check that field to the west.

(GROANING)

Jack, you believe this shit?

Stop. Stop, you're gonna
fuck it up even more.

All right. You ready?

- One, two, three.
- (SCREAMS)

Jack, Jack. I tried, man.

Don't worry about it. Don't worry about it.

Let's get you out. Let's get you out.

Get me up.

(GRUNTING)

Can you walk?

Yeah. Help me out. Help me out.

I'm coming!

(GROANING)

Dave, Dave, hey, I'm on your side.
Don't shoot me.

(DAVE GROANING)

TIG: It's okay, It's okay.
I got it, I got it!

I'll be right back. Yeah.

I want to live.

- Yeah. I'm coming right back.
- Don't!

My pistol, I need my pistol.

- Give me my pistol.
- Okay.

- Here we go. Here we go.
- (COCKING)

Men are on the way, all right?
Hang in. Hang in.

(GROANS)

JACK: Glen. Glen.

(GROANING)

God, watch over him.

Guide him where he needs to be.

Take care of his family.

OZ: Chief.

Dave's hurt really bad. (PANTING)

Get somebody up there to see him.

Rone, we need you
in medical immediately. Over.

CHIEF: Answer! Rone!

Rone's not with us anymore.

Oz, how can I help?

Get me to medical.

TIG: Dave's gonna bleed out fast
if you don't get up here.

I'm gonna need some tourniquets.

SONA: Clear that table back there.

Put pressure on that wound.

Get me naked. Check for bleeds.

Okay.

Trauma shears, top shelf on the right.

(GROANING)

Hey, hey, hey. Careful, careful, careful.

I don't want to get stabbed, too.

(DAVE GROANING)

What are you doing? No! No, no, no!

Hey! It's not the time!

(SCREAMING)

The enemy is still out there!

Let's go!

I called for air support.

It never came.

(GROANING)

GRS JOOST: Show it to me.

I lost the Ambo, man.

GRS JOOST: Are you allergic to morphine?

I lost the Ambo, Dave. What do I do?

Shut up and go get a gun on that door.

- (GROANS)
- Now!

(VEHICLES APPROACHING)

KRIS: You hear that, Boon? You hear trucks?

Chief.

Are we expecting any friendlies?

Oh, my God.

I got 40, 50 vehicles, including technicals.

I don't know.

KRIS: It's over, guys. It's fucking over.

A fucking massive heavy force.

Cock it, cock it.

As far as I'm concerned,
this isn't over till it ends.

That's when they're all dead or we are.

Oh, Lord! Oh, Jesus!

Guys, I think they're with us. (PANTING)

They're with us!

(TANTO LAUGHING)

They're with us! (LAUGHING IN RELIEF)

(SOBBING)

Oh!

Move, move!

(INDISTINCT CHATTER)

ALEC: It's not safe out here. Keep going.

SONA: Hurry! Get in the trucks!
They could still be coming.

Come on, guys, get in the trucks.

Come on. It's not safe out here.
Come on. Let's go.

Up, up, up! Please, please, please.

ALEC: Come on, guys!

Chief, it's time.

No, I'm staying.

Sir, this is the last ride out.

Yeah, I know. I'm staying.
I've got intel to collect.

Okay. Let's go!

What's the hold-up?

Your Chief, he won't exfil!

KRIS: It's not safe out here!

- You what?
- I've got work to do.

I'm staying.

For what?

So that more guys like Ty and Glen
have to come back here?

And save your ass again?

You're done here.

(WHISPERING) Now, get in the fucking car!

(BARKING)

KRIS: Amahl.

We made it, man.

Come on, get in the truck.

- I'm going home.
- What?

I'm so sorry.
This should never have happened.

Hey.

Your country's
got to figure this shit out, Amahl.

- (CAR DOOR CLOSING)
- (ENGINE STARTING)

(CAR DOOR CLOSING)

(OZ GRUNTS)

I walked into this country, I'm walking out.

Thank you.

I don't know how you survived all that.

But I know how the rest of us did.

You guys did well tonight.

I'm proud to know Americans like you.

Couple more hours till our plane.

Ambassador's body's just about here.

Hi, sir.

Can I have car?

Yeah.

(ALL CHEERING)

There's no way.

No way those mortars found us by chance.

Had to be set up on us days or weeks ago.

Listen.

Any other six guys,
I don't think we'd make it.

I think we were meant
to be together last night.

How do you think

the Chief's eval is gonna go?

He's going to get a medal. You'll see.

BOON: And the Deltas?

Yep. Medals. All of them.

TIG: And what about us?

The odds were 1,000-to-1, easy.

What do we get?

We get to go home.

KRIS: Libyan transport.

Still no Americans.

JACK: Hey.

It's me.

I wanted you to hear it from me first.
We had a...

A problem here.

Whatever you hear on the news, it's over now.

I'm done.

I'm coming home.

For good.

No.

No, I'm just lucky. I...

I'm just lucky.

(SOBS) He didn't make it.

Rone's not coming home.

I love you so much.

TYRONE: "All the gods, all the heavens,
all the hells are within you."

JACK: What is that?

TYRONE: Something Boon dropped on me earlier.

It's just been rattling around
in my head all night.

Printed in Great Britain
by Amazon

21830804R00078